Reviews of MEMW

"Holy S*@%, you gave me goosebumps...you put into words a lot of the things I've gone through. I'm excited to read more, keep writing!!!" — Jon

"Why didn't you tell me this book would make me cry... You're nicer than me; that @$$hole would've got punched in the face at Lowe's!" — Destiny

"It's really raw. It opened my eyes to a lot of things and I learned some things I didn't know about you." — Tye

"Auuuuhhhhmmaaaazzziiinnngggg! I loved it! Wonderful, wonderful job! So much truth! Breaks my heart, though." — Meranda

"I do have the sudden urge to go to the main gate now just to say "stay cool." — Amanda

MEMWARS
A Story of Survival

MEMWARS
A Story of Survival

Wendy M. Rodgers

FRANKLIN
SCRIBES™
PUBLISHERS

Franklin Scribes Publishing

Copyright © 2018 by Wendy Rodgers

All rights reserved. No part of this book may be used or reproduced in any manner whatsoever without the written permission of the author.

Rodgers, Wendy
Memwars/ A Story of Survival
ISBN 978-1-941516-35-5
First Edition
A Memoir

Library of Congress Control Number: 2018957208
ISBN Paperback: 978-1-941516-35-5
ISBN Ebook: 978-1-941516-36-2

Published by Franklin Scribes Publishers.
Franklin Scribes is a registered trademark
of Franklin Scribes Publishers.
Editor: Judy Sheer Watters sheermemoirs@gmail.com

franklinscribeswrites@gmail.com
www.franklinscribes.com

Contact the author at
www.franklinscribes.com/wendy-rodgers/
www.facebook.com/Wendy-M-Rodgers-Author-591170564374429/
wendymrodgersdotcom.wordpress.com/

Front and back book covers by Thompson Printing Solutions
This book was printed in the United States of America.

Table of Contents

Prologue: Identity Crisis   2017

Chapter 1: Summer Sadness   2017

Chapter 2: Method to my Madness   2006

Chapter 3: Do Not Pass Go!   2014/2015

Chapter 4: When Failure Demands Change   2005

Chapter 5: Integrity First!   2005

Chapter 6: Eye Openers   2006

Chapter 7: Going Deeper   2006/2007

Chapter 8: Domestic Enemy Number One   2015

Chapter 9: Last Ride of Freedom   2005

Chapter 10: "'Ten Hut!"   2005

Chapter 11: The Show Must Go On   2017

Chapter 12: Damn, How Do You Really Feel?   2017

Chapter 13: From Trainee to Airman   2006

Chapter 14: A Little Bit of Freedom   2006

Chapter 15: Guess Where You're Going   2006

Chapter 16: Back and There Again   2007/2008/2009

Chapter 17: You're Not Ready for This   2010/2014/2017

Chapter 18: Some 'Splaining to Do   2014/2017

Chapter 19: When Change Causes Failure   2017

Chapter 20: A Change in Scenery   2018

Chapter 21: In Conclusion

Epilogue: But What About Love?

Acknowledgments

Some Security Forces "Humor"

**I am not afraid to die, but I would fight to live…
Seriously, I will beat your ass if I have to.**

—A very wise person said after many margaritas—

Prologue: Identity Crisis

No need for introductions, here. The name's listed smack-dab on the front of this thing. I will address my title though. Scratch that—my many titles.

Before anything else, I am first, a child of God. Not to lead you to believe that I'm super-strong in my faith. On the contrary, I am very weak in that area. I just firmly believe that God deserves the first fruits in all things. Including how I identify myself.

Secondly, I am a mother, but I wasn't that before I became something else that I would always be. Don't get me wrong; being a mother is the best privilege I've ever had, but something came before that. Something that came before a lot of things for the rest of my life.

I am a Veteran. A war Veteran. A combat Veteran. Notice how only "Veteran" is capitalized? It's because that word means so much to me.

Why? Because dammit, it's the one I'm most proud of. I gave a lot for that word. I gave myself. All of myself. Whether I wanted to or not. And there's no greater truth in my life than that. And what's crazy, most important and maybe idiotic, is that I would do it again. And again. A million times over. Because as damaged as I am today, at least it wasn't for me. I didn't become someone else because of a selfish decision I made. In fact, it was the most selfless decision a person could make.

Yeah, I may have been running away from home in a sense, but is there a better reason to completely abandon the person you used to be than for your country?

If you're one of those super-radical Christians, you might say, "Yes, you heathen. For your Lord and Savior who gave His life for you." Well, as a Christian, I have to say, you might be right, but I reserve the right to ask you, "Would Jesus fault you for being proud that you sacrificed yourself for your nation? Your friends and family? Hell, strangers you don't even know who see you as less than scum because your skin is a little darker?" "Oh no, not the race card," said every non-dark person in unison with an eye roll.

I'm not saying I'm Jesus, people, but don't fault me for having pride in the sacrifices I've made. Because serving means you'll never ever be the same. The innocent or shitty life you knew before gets crucified, because it's not who they want you to be. And years, not days later, you are resurrected as someone you eventually don't recognize. The difference is, you are no Savior.

You are the one who needs saving.

This book is about a veteran who is trying to live a "normal" life after the wars. "Wars" plural, because of course there is the physical-real-world-war (say that 5x's real fast) and then there's the much worse, mental-forever-at-war-with-your-own-thoughts-and-decisions-war.

I hope this can also serve as a somewhat ray of hope for all the outsiders who are suffering and struggling through everyday life after traumatic events. Trying to fit in where and with whom you don't. Those who honestly believe that there is no one else who can relate.

MEMWARS : A STORY OF SURVIVAL

CHAPTER 1

Summer Sadness 2017

"Andreas?"

As I expected, there is no response. Except for maybe a twitch of my nine-year-old son's nose.

"Andreas," I try again. This time, a little more insistent because, you see, I have lollygagged all morning before work waiting for Good Morning America's Thursday " Deals & Steals" specials, and now it's my son's turn to take the blame for my tardiness for work.

I continue my summer morning ritual of telling my only child that I am 1) going to work, 2) his bowl, cereal and generic brand of chewable multivitamin are waiting for him on the table for when he wakes up, 3) he'd better not leave a mess on said table when he's done eating, 4) to stay away from the windows and doors, as well as to answer all of my calls/texts promptly, and 5) to text me as soon as he wakes up. Yes, yes, people, and that I love him also. Sheesh...

Finally, he sleepily acknowledges what I've said and rolls back over to sleep. I kiss my son on his crusty little drooled-upon cheek and secure the rest of the house.

I take very superficial comfort that I am doing the right thing by leaving him at home.

As I'm backing out of the driveway, I call him on the cell phone that I'd placed next to him while he was sleeping. You know, to make sure he remembered what I'd said. After a few groggy "Yes, Ma'am's," I am somewhat satisfied enough to hang up the phone.

Geez, paranoid much?

Yes…very much, thank you.

* * *

Two hours later, I had finished a couple of pedicures and checked my phone to see if my little rascal had messaged me.

Nope.

"Hey, Andreas isn't answering my calls or texts. Would you mind if I go home real fast to make sure he's okay," I asked, trying my absolute best to not sound as desperate as I felt.

I'm sure my boss thinks I'm nuts and I haven't even been working at her nail salon for long, but she says it's totally cool, and I practically run out to my car and speed home to check on him.

On the entire drive back home, I formulate a game plan. A course of action in case things have gone terribly wrong, as I imagine they have.

Within ten minutes, I turn off the ignition and tread carefully towards my front door. It's hard to listen for any noise out of the ordinary because my dogs have already recognized the sound of my car and are barking crazy loud. While holding my breath, I enter my house to find the television tuned into what I assume was a marathon of "Teen Titans Go!" and my son on the sofa, pajama-clad, with an expression of sheer confusion because, as I mentioned earlier, I'd only been gone for two hours.

But before he can even say "Hi, Mom," the smile on his face melts away as I'm already demanding to know why he hasn't answered any of my calls or texts. Turns out, his phone was on vibrate.

Nice one, Mom. You forgot to turn up the volume...

Before I leave again, I perform a "test" call and text to make sure he can hear both.

For the second time that day, I set off to work.

CHAPTER 2

Method to my Madness 2006

"Rodgers! Rodgers, wake UP!"

"Huh," I replied sleepily as I realized I'd fallen asleep watching Lord of the Rings: The Twin Towers on my portable DVD player.

It was nighttime and through uncorrected vision, I couldn't see our highest-ranking female Airman, but I recognized her voice. It was the first time I'd heard confusion, panic and fear all at once, but it damn sure wouldn't be the last.

"Rodgers, we're under attack! Take COVER!"

Then I remembered where I was. Tallil Air Base, Iraq, about a year after I'd enlisted in the United States Air Force.

I quickly rolled off my bed and laid down on the tent floor and instantly had to pee.

Come on, I can't be the only person in the world whose first reaction after getting out of bed is to relieve herself? No takers?

Stick around and I'll show you how wrong you are.

Most people might think that in the face of life and death, your survival instincts kick in. That the good ol' adrenaline takes over and you just know what to do. Well, that had been my first insurgent attack and all I felt was confusion and the desperate urge to pee.

"I have to use the latrine," I yelled to her as alarms and booms could be heard over my common sense.

"You can't leave. Stay down."

What's funny is she didn't even sound upset or annoyed. Just afraid.

Turns out, my dirtbagginess (laziness) from earlier that day prevented me from throwing away an empty water bottle. So I did what any self-respecting person would do.

I peed in that bottle and only then was my mind completely clear.

I could now think clearly enough to grab my gear and put it on, which was of course, within arm's reach. Even better, I could now think to get underneath my twin bed for better cover. And I could hear our phone ringing insistently, surely the higher-ups attempting to check our status, but neither of us dared to get up from our position of cover. Even though our landline was only fifty feet away from our location, it was much safer to stay right where we were.

When the attack was over, we both made sure that the other was okay and the Senior Master Sergeant called the squadron to let them know that we were fine.

I remembered my yucky pee bottle and once the all-clear alarm could be heard, I quickly rushed off to the latrine to throw it away.

On my way to destroy the evidence, I recalled a briefing we'd had upon our arrival. We had been warned beforehand that it was absolutely prohibited to pee in bottles in our tents. When I first heard this rule, I thought it was gross. I mean, why in the hell would someone be so lazy that they'd resort to peeing in a freaking water bottle?

Now I understood completely. And I knew without a doubt that I wasn't the only one whose principles had changed. Survival isn't always about fighting. The simple necessities of life take precedence over rules and regulations.

And they dared to tell us otherwise.

CHAPTER 3

Do Not Pass Go! 2014 – 2015

"Thank you for your interest in this position, but you are ineligible for employment due to your active warrant."

And that, ladies and gentlemen, is how I found out that I had become a criminal. Ever have the sensation of your heart falling straight to your stomach? Surely you have. I must've read that paragraph a thousand times before the reality of it sank in: I was going to jail.

And two weeks ago, I had just celebrated my 30th birthday.

Not long after that notification, there were some very loud bangs on my front door, followed by announcements of, "Abilene Police Department!"

Paralyzed by fear, I could not believe what was happening. I don't know how many there were, but they just kept pounding and pounding everywhere. It was like Iraq all over again. They pounded the front door, the windows, the sliding door.

Everywhere.

And I never opened the door. I waited for them to leave.

My son, who was only seven at the time, was petrified and inconsolable. I'm not sure if I cried or not. I just know that I was afraid, but about twenty minutes after they'd left, I went to the police station and turned myself in, leaving my son with "friends." I recited numbers to myself so I'd remember them for that damned phone call. And while I was behind a cell for three hours waiting for bail, I remembered the events that took me there.

One year prior, for some dumbass reason, I allowed my home to be taken over by the worst in-laws known to mankind. There were nine people living in my three-bedroom, one-bathroom house. Oh, and also a dog from hell that destroyed my freaking patio set.

So the place where I once found sanctuary from the world had now become the last place I wanted to be. Every single day was hell and what's worse is there wasn't even any help given on their part where it counted. After we'd been sucked up dry, they finally got the hell out of my house, but the damage had already been done.

I was angry. And dangerously so. Which led me to commit a crime.

Injury to a child.

Because I decided to defend the innocence of two helpless children who were put in a very compromising position by another child. Albeit, I shouldn't have reacted the way I did, but that's what happens when you have years and years of unchecked, pent-up anger without treatment. And I already hated that kid because he hated my kid and I would do anything to protect my kid.

Understand?

"Do you realize you're wearing a shirt that says "Go to Jail," one of the female jail guards asked incredulously, bringing me back to reality.

"Trust me, the irony is not lost on me," I replied wryly.

As I sat in the Taylor County jail, I felt like a huge failure. I was probably the shittiest individual in the entire world. I no longer had the right to be proud of my service to this country. Look at what I'd become.

A freaking criminal.

As I sat there waiting to bail out, I listened to my other two cellmates flap their jaws like jail was the place to be. Of course, they tried to include me into their conversation, but I just gave one-word responses and they finally got the hint. One got up to pee and the rest of my dignity was history after that.

Gals and guys, I tried so hard to hold it, but once again, like in Iraq, nature took over.

I took my sorry ass over to that toilet and peed.

I find it ironic that eight years prior, when I had no choice but to "break the rules" and pee in a bottle, I did so without hesitation, but while I was desperately trying to hold my pee in a jail cell and there was a toilet right there, I fought it with everything I had.

I got processed, fingerprinted, and "mugshot," and was eventually given my phone call.

Phone calls, actually.

They give you two; one for the bail bondsman you choose and the other for whoever is bailing you out. And how the hell was I supposed to know which bail service to choose? I must've looked pretty distraught because the lady monitoring the phones showed me some Christ-like grace and favor that I was not worthy of. Thanks, J.C.

"Do you need help," she kindly asked me.

"I'm not sure which one to call," I replied, about to cry.

"This one is pretty good from what I've heard," she said, and I chose the one she pointed to.

And do you know they didn't even answer the phone?

I could feel the anxiety going up another million degrees as I panicked, thinking that was it. No more phone privileges.

"Ma'am, they didn't answer the phone." I'm 98% sure that I was crying by then.

"Go ahead and try another one, Sweetie."

And so I did, and thank God, someone answered.

I placed my other call (to the one who's supposed to bail you out) and was escorted back to my cell. I had no idea what time it was because my watch, along with everything else, save the ironic tee and sweatpants I had on, had been collected. After what seemed like forever, I was finally freed on bond and spent the night at home, still feeling like a prisoner. As I was leaving, the observant female jailer I'd spoken to earlier made me promise that I would throw that stupid-ass t-shirt away.

And, yes, the hell, I did, in case you were wondering.

Also, one of my fellow jail mates asked me to call someone for them when I was leaving so they could get bailed out too. I actually did. I recited the number she gave me in my head over and over. But whoever it was didn't answer.

Sorry, Ma'am.

I didn't pick up my son that night. I was too ashamed to be a mother. Too ashamed to call myself a child of God, and definitely too damned ashamed to call myself a Veteran, as I so proudly did in the beginning of this book.

I was scum and no one could tell me differently.

Every knock on the door after that night was a threat. Every slam of a car door I heard from outside was surely that of an angry police officer coming back for me. I kept my blinds closed and hardly went anywhere.

I spoke to only one friend and if it hadn't been for her continuing to treat me like a human being, and dragging me out of my house, I would've been a complete recluse.

Thank you, Jeanette, AKA Hummie, for being there. I'll love you forever for being there for me when I needed somebody the most. You were the only person who did not turn their back on me.

Anyways, I had been given a court-appointed attorney, a court date, a sentence of two years of probation with forty hours of community service, and an adult babysitter, AKA probation officer.

During my first meeting with her, she asked me the silliest question I'd heard in a long time.

"So...excuse me, but what the hell are you doing here?"

"Ma'am?"

"How is it possible that you're sitting here? You seem too normal to be here. I have your file right here, but I need to know how you ended up on probation."

So, I explained to her the events that had transpired that brought my sorry self to her office, but she still seemed uncertain.

She brushed it off, though, and we went into the rules that would govern my life for the next two years.

No drinking, no associating myself with other known criminals, no staying out past curfew (midnight, lest I turn into a pumpkin), no attendance at any bars, clubs, honky-tonks (I swear to God, it really said "honky-tonks"), no traveling to certain places without, get this, permission to travel via travel voucher, and many others I don't remember.

With good behavior, consistent clean pee tests, completed community service, and all court fees paid, I was released a year early. But in that year, I was given another adult babysitter who, believe it or not, asked me the same silly question as the first one.

* * *

"I have a confession," my first probation officer said a year later when we met for coffee so she could edit my first attempt at a book.

"What do you mean?" I asked.

"I asked about you when I was your officer. I had to check you out."

"What do you mean?" I was completely caught off guard because how could we possibly have anyone in common?

"I asked my ex-husband," she replied simply, taking a sip of whatever she'd ordered.

Now I knew she was joking because I didn't know her ex, and I told her as such.

But then she said his name and my mouth must've fallen straight to the floor!

"Omg, he's your ex? No freaking way!"

"Yep, and he was surprised to hear that you had gotten into trouble. He said you were always a sharp troop."

Yep, he was an old supervisor from my old squadron! Small world, Abilene, TX.

"Wow, I can't believe that. Wait – so he knows," I asked, suddenly panicked.

"Well, I had to tell him why I was asking. And no, he's not telling the squadron."

When we first met, I asked her if I had to tell my leadership, and she'd said "I won't tell if you don't."

And I found out that there were lots of members in the military (I didn't know who, of course) who had also run into some legal issues. I still felt shitty for my choices, but I didn't feel as alone in them anymore.

If you can understand that, you're the one I'm writing this book for. Someone who can understand what you're going through can be that last little bit of hope you need.

And if you can understand me, then you can be damn sure that I get you.

CHAPTER 4

When Failure Demands Change 2005

"Mom?"

Extremely fearful of my next words, yet I knew deep down, even beyond the defiance behind them, that I needed to say them.

The woman I'd called my mother since I was about eight years old was watching the five o'clock news in the spacious living room of our very well-decorated two-story home in one of many cul-de-sacs in Palmdale, California.

"What is it, Wendy?" She was slightly annoyed, and rightly so, because honestly, I could've waited for a commercial break. There was no breaking news on, but still, I could've waited.

"I think I want to join the military."

With this statement, I had her full attention because she just stared at me. Not right away, but in that just right amount of time when moms have processed what their child has said and aren't really sure if that's really what they heard.

Then she stared the way a parent does when they're looking for the truth in their child's eyes. She was looking for a seriousness that only comes at the age when life has been met at that proverbial "crossroads." I guess that day, she saw that truth in my eyes. Her serious expression changed, although very slightly. It was enough for me to continue with the words that would change my life forever.

"I've thought about it a lot, and I think this is what I need to do." My voice was weak, but the conviction in my words was strong. For the past two years, after graduating from Highland High School, I had been living at home. Still.

Towards the end of senior year, I had been accepted into a few Cal State colleges, with only one condition: I had to pass a chemistry course over the summer. It's what they call a "conditional acceptance," kids. Take that shit seriously.

Anyway, despite my excitement over getting into college, I was destined to fail. And in the most epic way. And for the dumbest reason, too. How, you asked? Well, because in the year 2003, during that fateful summer, the death of my would-be college experience arrived in the forms of two television shows: "America's Next Top Model" and "The O.C." Holy Crap! I can remember them like it was just yesterday. But whatever, I digress.

Needless to say, I failed the lecture portion of that God-forsaken chemistry course at my local community college because, get this: I often left an hour early to go home and watch my shows! There was no DVR or TiVo then, so it was either set your VCR's (I've never had any technological abilities) or be super cool and skip class to watch your favorite-oh-so-important-unimportant shows. It should've come as no surprise when that transcript came in, crushing all of my dreams of attending Cal State San Bernardino, class of 2007.

But it did.

Instead, the year 2007 would hold an entirely more meaningful milestone for me. Of course, I didn't know that at the time, but all I felt was my first pang of raw disappointment in myself. You'd think that even visiting the campus with my mother would be enough motivation to ensure my acceptance, but no. Not yet, at least. I would not know true motivation until later in life.

But where was I? Oh, yeah, the conversation that "forever changed me." Sorry, guys, I should've mentioned the short attention span that has now, like so many other things, frazzled my brain.

"You don't have to join the military to leave home, you know." Her words sounded a little bitter, but she was onto something. I hated that she knew everything, but it was true.

"I'm not just trying to leave home, Mom," I semi-whined, although I totally was. "I'm not old enough to be a cop yet, and I don't see any other option. Working at

Hallmark cards isn't enough to get my own place, and I hate school."

Although my words had logic behind them, she was no fool. It was true, we had been bumping heads ever since I'd turned eighteen and I thought I was grown. She only had two rules if any of us five kids were to stay at home after turning eighteen: either go to school or have a job. Plus, I was paying "rent" so, silly me, I thought that made us equals. Wrong! I thought that she would never see me as the adult I desperately wanted to be as long as I still lived under her roof. I needed to leave and prove it to her and myself.

And the military seemed like the best route to go. Besides, I learned all I needed to know from four years of AFJROTC, right? Ha! Man, I was a real dummy back in the day. Like anything has changed.

"Okay, Wendy. We'll talk more about this later," she said, cool and calm as could be, but I could tell she wasn't all that "cool" with our would-be future discussions.

"Yes, Mom." Phew! I let out a silent breath of relief, as that first hurdle was cleared. The fact that she hadn't laughed or bit my head off was enough for me.

Now the real fun was just about to begin.

CHAPTER 5

Integrity First! 2005

A couple of weeks later, after much back and forth, my mom finally realized that I was "for real" about enlisting. Through discussions of "not-the-Army-because-you're-sure-to-deploy," I assured my overprotective mother that I had already chosen the Air Force and was ready to call my local liar.

My bad, recruiter.

I will admit now that I remember being scared shitless making that phone call. I remember the guy was a sergeant of some kind. Anyway, I made an appointment to see "Sergeant-of-some-kind" and let my mom know so we could go together. You know, in case they lied to me. So freaking hilarious because, OF COURSE, he lied to me!

Let's go ahead and fast forward to that meeting...

After my mom parked in one of the approved Armed Forces Recruiting parking spaces, I put on my game face as we made our way to the entrance. My mother and I made no eye contact as we walked away from my last hope for stopping the catastrophe-that-was-to-be. That last hope being the family car to escape back to the safety of my home. Duh.

Anyway, we both had something to prove that day: on my end, that I was seriously doing this, and on hers, that she was letting me "prove this point."

I don't remember exactly what was said once we walked through the door, but naturally we were swarmed by Navy, Army, and Marine recruiters all at once. Yes, Marines too. Despite the popular belief or rumor that Marine recruiters wait to be approached. Believe it or not, it's actually the "Chair" Force that makes you wait.

So yes, we're finally greeted by my Air Force liar. Recruiter. Geez, I've really got to stop doing that. Especially since I almost become one myself years later. Turns out, I had too much pride and integrity.

Go figure.

Staff Sergeant So-and-So will be the name of the man that uttered all of the untruths to me as I began the process of signing my life away. My mother and I (mostly me, because she wouldn't be the culprit in this decision) asked questions that seemed relevant at the time.

"What about deploying? To Iraq?" my mom asked after, I suppose, she could no longer remain silent.

At the time, troops going to Iraq and Afghanistan were all over the news ever since September 11th. Even four years later. It wouldn't have been a deal-breaker for me if I had to go. Actually, the thought of going was kind of exciting, because then I knew for sure I'd be worth something. The foreboding, yet distant voice in the background saying "Careful what you wish for" would not be heard at this time.

"Well, Ma'am. There is absolutely no chance of your daughter deploying because that's just not the Air Force's mission right now. I myself was K-9. Check these out."

Looking back now, I'm pretty sure that's what we would call a diversion: "Hey look, pictures!"

Anyway, this is the part where he showed me pictures of him and his MWD (Military Working Dog) sitting on a stack of what my then untrained eyes were supposed to recognize as explosives. In what looked like a desert area...

"Doesn't that look cool to you?" Staff Sergeant Liar excitedly searched my face for some kind of agreeable confirmation.

My smart ass replied, "Well, to me it just looks like a German Shepherd lying down." In truth, what I saw took me back to an event that had occurred no more than a month before.

My mother and I were the only ones home when we had to take our ten-year-old German Shepherd, Kajun, to be euthanized. A once very energetic dog, that would bark for absolutely no reason and annoy us all, had come to a point where her teeth had ground down and she couldn't even eat dry food, much less move. In fact, her organs had eventually turned outside of her body. The car ride was both foul-smelling and very heartbreaking. She just laid there, in the back of our family minivan and took her final ride.

The dog in the picture looked just like Kajun, but I didn't tell SSgt So-and-So the hurtful memories that his career brought to my mind. And why should I? He was genuinely proud. As well he should've been. But that would be the first, although not the last, time that I had decided to suppress my feelings instead of meeting them head on. Looking back, I was already conditioning myself for a world of internal pain that I would share with very few individuals.

So, after countless meetings and appointments, I enlisted for four years of Active Duty service. My mother probably wouldn't have allowed it if she'd had the choice. I went through MEPS (Military Entrance Processing Station) and on the second trip, raised my right hand and swore to defend the United States of America from enemies both foreign and domestic.

CHAPTER 6

Eye Openers 2006

So, there I was. At Tallil Air Base, Iraq, with my team and my buddies. I must admit, I felt super cool being there. Like some bad-ass just because of a location.

Plus, I had some good times there; it wasn't all bad.

For instance, I remember one night, I was doing some online shopping and I couldn't decide between two pairs of shoes in the exact same style, just different colors. So I had to phone home, have my mom and sister get on the same website to help me decide on which pair. Also, I got my first and only sunburn in Iraq. Yes, walking to the DFAC, the entire left-side of my Black face got super sunburnt!

Shhhh, it's not racist if I say it...

Anyway, eventually we were given our living assignments, bedding, tent mates, job assignments, shifts. We got our addresses and calling cards so we could contact our loved ones back home. I reassured my mom that I was just fine and she had nothing to worry about.

Then, the real fun began.

It didn't even start with weapons of war. It began from

the inside.

With the leadership.

Most of us airmen were on our first deployment and had never experienced anything like this. With that being said, I guess it was only natural for a certain female Senior NCO (non-commissioned officer), the same one I would experience my first attack with, to take full advantage of that.

While my buddies and I were being goofy and helping each other decorate "rooms" in our tent, this sorry excuse for a leader takes it upon herself to take us under her wings.

"I just want you guys to know that I'm here for you if you ever need to talk. My door is always open for you. No questions asked." Some stupid shit like that, but of course, we didn't really know any better and totally, foolishly ate that shit right up.

So fast forward a little bit, and one of us actually decided to use her false "open door policy." It was the highest ranking of us four, the Senior Airman. She had been deployed once before, so maybe she should've seen this coming. But when a female SMSgt tells you that you can come to her if you need her, you're not completely wrong in wanting to believe her. I mean, Integrity First and all that. Especially in a career field where the good ol' boys look out for each other. Why can't we do the same?

Because women are catty bitches, that's why.

This airman takes the senior up on her offer and confides in her. She shares with her how she feels about the position she was given and how she'd been treated by males as a result. I'm sure the "confidante" reassured her that she would look into the matter and she need not worry.

PSYCH!!

One day, the other three of us were hanging out on a day off, slacking and snacking, and before we know it, here comes our buddy looking super-red-faced and on the verge of tears. After calming her down, we learned of the betrayal.

"What's wrong?" one of us asked.

"I got in trouble for jumping the chain of command," she replied, growing more emotional by the minute.

"What the hell happened?" someone was sure to have asked.

"Remember when the Senior said we could talk to her if we needed to?"

"Yeah…," we all replied, looking at each other uneasily.

"Well, last night at chow, she asked me how everything was going at work, so I told her."

"Okay…then what?" but we all kind of had an idea of

where it was going after that.

Apparently that open-door policy was just a trap to blindside our buddy's direct supervisor and make life a living hell for her. What this low-life senior did was lie and say that the airman had skipped her chain of command and ran crying to her about all the problems within their office. I won't get into all the details, but the backlash was abominable and very humiliating for our friend. You can't even imagine the betrayal we all felt at that point. So…we did what any group of true friends would do in that situation:

We completely ostracized that piece of shit SMSgt.

We never spoke to her other than a respectful "Yes, Ma'am" or "No, Ma'am." Eventually she got the picture, because I remember one night, I went back to my tent to retrieve something I forgot to bring to work. My tent mates and I were catching up a little bit while I was there (they worked days, I worked nights) and who invites herself into whoever's "room" it was, trying to get in on our conversation but Lady Judas?

We all stopped talking and looked at her, and I shit you not, she slumped her shoulders, hung her head, and said, "Yeah, I know," and left.

That's just one of the many internal incidents that happened while on my first deployment. The attacks from the inside aren't any less damaging from the ones on the outside.

Because there was no trust. And when it's a matter of life and death, trust is essential.

We should've been able to rely on each other, but that's not even close to how it was. There were always politics involved, when they should've been considering our humanity.

We had no one, but each other, and it turns out we didn't even have that.

You couldn't even have an airman from another base passing a test with a 90% and being happy for them without your own home base NCOs saying, "No, you need to do better than them. Do you want them to look better than us? Have you forgotten which base you've come from?"

Like, seriously? We're in Iraq, with way bigger priorities and you want me to compete with someone's score? And now you're questioning my loyalty because I said congratulations?

Alright, let's consider those rose-colored sunglasses good and lifted off this sunburnt face.

CHAPTER 7

Going Deeper 2006/2007

Well, now that you have a sprinkle of an idea of what we dealt with on the inside, I'll go further into the external side.

Before I experienced any sort of attack from terrorists, I would be forced to ponder another turn of events.

I was originally slotted to deploy to Afghanistan, but at the last minute, a few airmen were switched around. Well, that just may as well have been God looking out for my wack ass.

One day, we were all told to show up to a mandatory formation in Tent City for a briefing. None of us low-ranking airmen knew what it was about, or why we couldn't be asleep if we happened to be on a mid-shift schedule and working later that night.

To summarize things, we were informed that we had lost a fellow airman deployed to Afghanistan. I don't remember what his name was, but I remember that he was around my age, same career field – a Security Forces troop. We had our Moment of Silence and anyone who needed to speak with a chaplain was allowed to do so.

Without sounding like the most selfish piece of garbage on the planet, I couldn't help but wonder if that could've been me. What if I was switched at the last minute through God's design to save my life? I'm not saying that God took his life instead. I don't believe He takes life at all. Somewhere in the Good Book, it says that the other guy steals, kills and destroys. He did not take that young man's life. But what if that had been my mother receiving that phone call because that is where I was originally supposed to be?

I was no longer disgruntled about the sleep that I was robbed of because I had to show up to that formation. I mean, shit, I could've been sleeping eternally.

It didn't take long after that for us to start experiencing our own attacks from the enemy. I don't remember every single one, but I remember the first attack I've shared with you already and when we got lit the hell up after Saddam was assassinated. It was December 30, 2006. For days, insurgents retaliated against us. It was mandatory to be in full-gear at all times.

Even to go to my beloved bathroom.

Another of those attacks I'll always remember because for most of us, like I said, it was our first deployment. I don't remember every shitty, nitty-gritty detail, but for the most part, everyone had to report to the armory for accountability. Everyone else who wasn't on duty and still in their tents, had to report in telephonically.

After all was said and done, and the "all clear" sounded, things wont "back to normal," but tensions were still very high. Whoever was still lingering in the armory was understandably still on edge and wanted to be around "their people." But you know what the effed-up thing was? Anytime we heard a loud thud or bang after that, one particular person who had been deployed before, laughed at whoever was jumpy.

As if they were scaredy-cats for being afraid for their lives.

Just moments ago, we were all scared shitless, but after the fact, it's a joke for such a traumatic event to have you shaken up? When I saw that, in the vulnerable state that I was in, instead of standing up for that person's feelings, I stifled my fears and pretended like it (the attack) didn't bother me.

It was the worst possible thing I could've done and it set the tone for the rest of my Air Force career.

Why? Because I learned that there is a stigma about confessing to PTSD. If you admit to it, you could lose your Secret Clearance, therefore, making you non-deployable, therefore, useless to the Air Force, therefore, leaving you jobless. So, you don't say anything because of a new fear: losing what you worked so hard for in the first place.

Also, the fear of looking like a weakling who couldn't

handle the job.

There were other times scattered throughout the rest of that deployment, but the last significant event was the journey out of there.

The beginning of the end.

We had to travel in full gear, in a convoy from Tallil Air Base to the airport where we were to fly out of because we could've been attacked while in transit. That last ride could very well have been our last ride period. And not just that. What about the Army soldiers who were driving those Rhinos and tanks to get us airmen safely to our destination? Who was going to protect them once they were on their way back? And do they hate us for getting out of there, while they had to stay? When it's their turn to leave, will their convoy be as diligent in keeping them out of harm's way?

I regret that at the time I was not thinking about those soldiers. I was thinking, "Thank God we made it. And if you still love me, God, please get me all the way home."

But that's what the mindset of survival is.

I feel horrible for not praying for their safe trip back home right then and there. Maybe if teamwork had been the focal point of the tour, I wouldn't have been focused solely on my own survival. We were all brothers and sisters-in-arms. I should've been thinking about all of our outcomes.

From the start, we had to look out for ourselves.

But, believe me, when those travel bans hit in the summer of 2017, I know in my heart that whoever was deployed to a combat zone was feeling the wrath of those radical terrorists. I prayed then and I've been praying ever since after the first return home.

Well, we did make it back. Obviously. We landed in Baltimore, Maryland. And do you know what almost everyone did that night in celebration?

GOT DRUNK!

And is that any surprise? It shouldn't be. But what is surprising, is that combat vets don't just celebrate happy occasions with alcohol. We drown those fears, regrets, sorrows, and true selves in alcohol. Hell, yeah, we were happy we made it back to the States, but our minds would forever be somewhere else. Always ready for that other shoe to drop no matter where we were.

But for some of us, at least for me, everything comes back in full-force with a drink or two. I remember most of it as if it had just happened yesterday. Truth be told, it's how I'm able to write this book so effectively.

Yep, that's right; you're mostly reading my drunken memories. But don't worry, everything was verified by a fellow airman. What I'm telling you is true, I just had to use unsavory means to tell you my story.

The war overseas was only the beginning. The real war would be realized much later in life. For some of us, like me, when it was too late.

CHAPTER 8

Domestic Enemy Number One 2015

"Okay, now that we've all rolled perms together, you guys go ahead and repeat the procedure on your own mannequins. I'll be back in about fifteen minutes to check your work."

It was chemical mock week in cosmetology school and the six of us juniors set off to hone our hairstyling skills while the seniors began taking clients or working on their dailies. I still have one or two pairs of the purple scrubs we had to wear for a year from those days.

The demonstration from our instructor had been semi-formal since we were such a small group and most likely, so we could be more comfortable with our surroundings and each other. We had all laughed and joked about how easy we thought it was while following her instructions. It was a welcome relaxed setting after years of "sit down and color" antics.

So far, I was enjoying cosmetology school and I had hit it off with at least one other student from day one.

"Girl, this is way harder than it looks," I said. "I can barely wrap the hair tight enough!"

"Me, too, I'm gonna take a quick smoke break. My fingers already hurt."

We all laughed, and as my new friend took off, I went back to practicing on my mannequin. I looked around at everyone else's work and noticed that the only male in our group was doing a really good job on his faux-client.

"Wow, that looks really good! How'd you get yours rolled up so tight?"

"Maybe if you all weren't so busy talking, yours could be too," he'd replied in a very matter-of-fact tone.

Ladies and gentlemen, I had a choice at that moment. I could've handled that comment like an adult, or like an ignoramus with a very short fuse. After weeks of pretending to be a "good little girl," guess which route I took?

"WTF (not actually what I'd said) did you just say to me?" I asked about two seconds later, as I realized I was about to go full-on crazed bee-yotch.

After slight hesitation, he repeated himself. But this time, not as confidently.

"Who the eff (again, not what I said) do you think you are? I was just complimenting your punk ass! You don't freaking know me…"

The rant continued with all sorts of hand gestures, cuss words and me doing my best to keep my distance before

I went straight up all upside his head. The other juniors stood by and witnessed this dude getting cursed out and it went on with him getting very few words in until both instructors came by to see what the commotion was.

The one who'd taught us only moments before breaks it off and demands to know what the hell happened in the short time she was gone.

"This mother-effer (again, you know the drill) decided to act all big and bold and start talking shit like I'm not gonna say something." I continued to yell because I'm still super pissed and I had not yet said all that I needed to say.

As he stood there, basically at a loss for words, the instructor deemed that it was time for us all to go out back and have a "come to Jesus session."

We get outside, and she asks us all if there's anything we'd like to say to clear the air. Immediately, I shoot my hand up as I'm angrily pacing back and forth.

"I'll get to you last, Wendy. You need to cool off and listen while everybody else talks. Still fuming, I continue to pace. I am not listening to a word that anyone is saying.

My mind is racing.

Thoughts of: "WTF are you doing – this is your last shot – get your shit together before you end up back in jail – bitch, you're still on probation – you're better than this, you're a mom, act like it – but I'm no effing punk – who TF does he think he is," etc, run through my mind.

After what seems like an eternity, it's finally my turn to chime in. Albeit, this time I wasn't yelling. I had managed to calm myself down.

He ended up apologizing for his remark, but I wasn't ready to forgive. In fact, I didn't speak to him again for weeks. And he tried everything he could to fix it, from sharing or buying styling tools, to damn right being an overall more pleasant person. But it wasn't enough.

I had been wronged.

One of many things about me is that I can carry a grudge. For years, if "need" be. I can keep all the hurt and pain nestled up somewhere and release a tiny portion of it on some poor unassuming individual without a moment's notice.

"I didn't even know you could speak that way," the instructor said after everything was "resolved."

"Well, I am military and some habits are hard to kill."

She nodded as if she understood – but, how could she?

How could she know the shame I felt that I'd just exploded like that? That everyone now knew that I wasn't the "good girl" that I'd pretended to be?

Sure enough, most people were smart enough to not "mess with me" after that. There may or may not have been a few more run-ins after that one, but I will neither confirm, nor deny.

CHAPTER 9

Last Ride of Freedom 2005

It would be easy to say "I'll never forget that ride to Lackland Air Force Base in pursuit of BMT (Basic Military Training) for as long as I live," but truth be told, I only remember bits and pieces of it. I don't even remember getting off the plane and getting on the bus.

Anyway, I remember about four of the people who I went with on that final trip to MEPS. The most memorable is the one who would become my Air Force sister and with whom I would eventually get my first and only tattoo, and who would also be in my flight in basic training.

Yes, the bus ride to good ol' Lackland AFB, Texas! I remember feeling like I had finally conquered my life. That I was fully in control. HA! Have I mentioned before what a dummy I was?

I do slightly remember when that bus stopped once we got there. I'm pretty sure every soul on that bus felt the panicked feeling of "Holy crap! What the eff have I done?"

And then we all saw them.

Maybe not at the same time, but at some point, we all

stared wide-eyed in the same direction.

Four very scary-looking figures with crisp BDU's (Battle Dress Uniform) tailored to their physique, combat boots as black as night that clapped like thunder when they hit the ground, and that damned hat we've all come to know and love, tilted ever so slightly, so that the brim rested firmly just above their eyes.

And they were practically storming our way.

I believe the bus driver said something encouraging, but there was no way any of us could've heard what he'd said over the pounding of our own hearts. All of us on that bus knew, but at the same time didn't really know "what time it was," and ready or not, they were coming for us.

And freaking fast!

We all just sat and waited. I think a few people stood up, but thought better of it and nervously sat back down. The bus driver opened the door, letting down that last protective barrier shielding our childhood. Betraying us all. What a jerk.

Ever have that sensation where your mouth is totally dry and you can barely swallow your own spit for fear that you might choke? Sweet – then you know how we all felt!

"GET OFF THIS BUS, YOU FREAKING LAZY SORRY EXCUSES FOR TRAINEES," the first one bellowed.

"WHAT DO YOU THINK THIS IS? A FREAKING

SHUTTLE TO THE HOLIDAY INN? GRAB YOUR CRAP AND MOOOOOOVE," another shouted.

"YOU THINK I'M LETTING YOU INTO MY AIR FORCE? THINK AGAIN, TRAINEES," the third one chimed in.

And the fourth one just stood outside, arms crossed, feet set wide apart, and stared at us with the cruelest smirk I'd ever seen. He could've been drooling like a rabid dog too, for all I know!

And with that, our Air Force careers began.

CHAPTER 10

"'Ten Hut!" 2005

I vaguely remember the hustle and bustle after getting our asses chewed all the way from the bus to what would be our new homes for the next seven weeks. Even longer for those that got washed back to another flight for illness or bad behavior.

Before I knew it, males and females had gotten separated and sent to their respective training squadrons and we were suddenly in what we now know as the Day Room of our dormitory.

I'm not even sure it had windows, so I don't know why "Day Room" seemed appropriate. In fact, I'm sure it didn't, because I remember a time when one of the element leaders effed up royally and we got smoked pretty badly in that very room. There were mountain climbers, diamond push-ups and other fun activities galore on the menu that night. Yes, it was hot, sweaty and gross in there.

When we got to our dormitory at the 331st Training Squadron, (Wolfpack, HUA?!) the Day Room was already halfway filled with other females and once we sat down, they harshly whispered to us newbies that we needed to shut the eff up at all times (of course the Training Instructor wasn't in there yet) or suffer horrible consequences. They'd had a leg up on us because they'd arrived two days before.

By the way, because we were in the military now, the words "girls" or "boys" were no longer in our vocabulary.

My experience up to this point was very surreal. I know that I was scared out of my mind, and in no way could this really be happening. At any moment, I would wake up in my own room, make my bed, have breakfast and go back to work at my real job at Diane's Hallmark in the Antelope Valley Mall, thus effectively putting an end to this whole nightmare.

Nope! No such luck.

I don't really remember much from that first day, except that we had to put all of our luggage away in a utility closet and most of us would never see it again for another seven weeks. I can't even recall how I slept that night, but I sure remember hearing "Taps" for the first time, signifying that it was bedtime and harshly waking up to "Reveille" the next morning. And, I remember that my Air Force buddy from MEPS was in the bunk next to me and we pretty much carried each other through those rough times.

My first week of Basic Military Training was both scary and depressing. Okay, most of basic was that way, but especially that first week because I arrived the week of Thanksgiving. That seemed to have set the tone for the future, because the majority of my Active Duty service would have me engaged in duty overseas for the holidays.

I do, however, remember very well the first time I ever ate at the chow hall. The infamous DFAC (Dining Facility). Good Lord, what an experience! I probably lost ten pounds that first week out of sheer fear to eat!

I nervously waited in line, not knowing what to expect. Obviously, my fellow trainees felt that same fear, because you could cut the tension with a knife. Once we made it past the corridor into the actual chow line, the state of fear rose another ten notches. Our T.I. was in there watching and waiting, because God forbid we actually say something.

"Hurry up, Females! We don't have all day," he barked.

The fact that he sounded like Ricky Ricardo didn't make him any less scary.

Silently, while making no eye-contact whatsoever with anyone, we pointed to the food we wanted and side-stepped through the line, until it was time for another challenge:

Walking past the "Snake Pit."

"What's the Snake Pit, Wendy?" Glad you asked!

You know how at a wedding reception there's usually

a table of honor with the bride, groom, moms/dads, etc? Well, it's kind of like that, except it's not nearly as cheerful an event. The table is occupied by the T.I.s of each flight eating at that appointed time. And they are just waiting for some poor soul with the nerve to break their military bearing and look at them.

Some poor trainee did just that.

"GET OVER HERE, YOU!"

Those of us who knew better than to look in that direction, knew to keep on scurrying to the next available table and scarf down our food as quickly as humanly possible.

At minimum, every single T.I. let that trainee have it – front and center. None of us scared-shitless trainees watched, but we could hear it.

"You got something to say to me?" followed by "Who the hell do you think you are eyeballing me?" and threats like "You better keep holding that tray up or you'll be eating that food off my boots," and probably an "Are those tears I see?" just for grins and giggles.

On top of that, they got quizzed on crap about people and things none of us knew about, got yelled at some more, before getting sent back to the end of the line because they answered incorrectly.

Oh, and because they were foolish enough to have looked over there in the first place.

Once the rest of us were done swallowing down breakfast and liquids, we turned our cups upside down, got up and got the hell out before anyone could see all the spilled water or Gatorade in our trays.

Ah, those were the days!

Anyway, think you can handle that? Then hot damn! You are more than prepared to dine with the trainees at Lackland AFB anytime!

The rest of basic was pretty much a blur. At some point, we were given BDUs to wear every day and a few PT (physical training) uniforms for those glorious hours of fitness. Speaking of, there was physical training every day. I've always loved to run, so that portion wasn't really a problem. However, there were still rough days. I've actually never told anyone this, but whenever we ran outside, and I was having a tough time motivating myself (here's where that motivation I didn't have for college was making its debut), I always imagined myself running to my mom. Like she was there, waiting at the finish line, cheering me on. Corny, but we all needed something to get us through any or all of it. On the days we did not run, we had to do calisthenics. That shit was the absolute worst! I'm not even gonna go there, but we were some seriously tough ladies and gents by the time Warrior Week came up for fifth week!

Of course, we did drill, got more than our fill of vaccinations, fired weapons (a first for me) and continued to get "put on our faces" every time we messed up. I can still hear him now:

"Get on your face, Females! Up! Down! Halfway up! Up! Halfway down! Down! Recover!"

The reason behind all the harsh words were unknown to us at the time. For unbeknownst to us, they were stripping away the children of yesterday and transforming us into better, stronger individuals.

Another event in basic that I shan't forget is that first call home. Well, damn, if that wasn't a day to remember.

We all had calling cards that we had to use for the payphones (yes, payphones) on the patio to call our loved ones and little pieces of paper where we'd written something about us all being fine and our address for care packages.

You could feel the anticipation in the air on that day, because it had been weeks since any of us had heard a kind or loving word from "the outside." Sure, we encouraged each other the best we could, but that just was not enough.

As we all waited in line to make our first calls home, I remember telling myself "Do not cry! You can do this. You can be strong. Do not cry on that damn phone!"

Even though I'd watched my fellow brothers and sisters make their phone calls and walk away after the few minutes we were given in complete tears, I still resolved myself to be unbroken. What was worse, was that some of them couldn't even get through to their families and had tears in their eyes because they were still empty in a sense. There was maybe one or two who did not cry after their conversation was complete and I wanted to be one of them, so when it was finally my turn, I knew it was my moment to prove to myself and my mom that I had grown up.

And then I heard her oh-so-far-away voice on the other end of the line.

Unfortunately, I was so, so, so unprepared for that moment! There was nothing, not even an act of God that could've kept me from crying on that phone on that day. My only explanation for my little weak self was that the same wave of emotion had swept over nearly everyone upon hearing their loved one's voice. I don't remember everything I said, but I'm sure I read that stupid-ass mandatory-yet-somehow-legal ransom note and apologized a million times for crying and that I was okay even though I was crying. She could've been close to tears herself, but I just remember her voice. Still, over ten years later, I am embarrassed of that train wreck of a phone call!

But somehow, after that tearful conversation, I felt something in me change. I believe that is when anger reared its ugly head. I felt betrayed. It sounds very silly to feel that way after that tiny event, but I honestly felt betrayed because here I was trying my damnedest to become something more, and in the process, I was made to break my mother's heart. I hated that I cried, but even more so that I had no choice but to cry. How could I not? I had gone from being the happy-go-lucky young adult from So-Cal, to a broken, yet strangely stronger growing woman. I could feel myself transforming into something else. I knew deep down that the girl who had arrived only weeks before was slowly slipping away.

I hung up that phone, wiped the tears from my face, and walked away from that payphone jaw set, fists clenched and determined to not let the Air Force get the best of me again.

Yeah, right.

CHAPTER 11

The Show Must Go On 2017

We've all heard the term "monkey suit" when people refer to themselves as going to work. I understand the philosophy totally. You put on the so-called costume and slap a smile on your face to earn an honest dollar.

Well, it's a little different for the likes of me, because when I go to work, it's as if I'm shedding my entire self to fit in with everyone else. And the dollar doesn't feel "honest" at all.

I feel like a complete fraud.

I am still pretending to be someone I am not for the sake of merely appearing to be normal. Oh, and to pay the bills, of course.

The costume is the civilian clothes I put on in place of the Kevlar vest and helmet, tight-ass uncomfortable boots that destroyed any possibility of pretty Cinderella-like arches in my feet, my M-9 pistol and M-4 rifle. The enemy is still unknown because I never saw him or her in the first place. I only saw their hate for me in the form of indirect fire and warnings to take cover.

The state of mind is still survival.

Not knowing if this could still be the day you die takes a toll, but reminding yourself that you haven't been down-range in years, forces you to relax just a little bit. But then again, the enemy was never seen, so they could very well be close by. I don't know what they really and truly look like. I saw the faces of my leadership every day, but I didn't know until I had been bitten that they were snakes.

Still, in my world no one can be trusted. Everything is personal and absolutely no one understands.

Especially no civilian.

This is my everyday mantra and has been for over ten years. To this day, I don't trust trash on the side of the road. I might look at it and keep driving (quickly), but on the inside, I am reminding myself to not be complacent. Stay aware. Know your surroundings. Keep your head on a swivel, etc. One up, one down (one sleeps, one's awake/on-guard). Well, I am alone so I guess sleep isn't really an option. All the things that are drilled into the mind until the essence of living freely is gone.

Every time I go to work, it is a mental battle. What do I say? What do I wear? Maybe I'll say nothing. No, that would make me a weirdo. Do I pretend I didn't hear that? Do I act like I did? Do I relent and admit that I am not like you? Does it matter that I used to be?

No. Because that person is long-gone.

And I am all that's left.

You're quite welcome.

CHAPTER 12

Damn, How Do You Really Feel? 2017

As I pull into work every Tuesday morning, I think about the counseling I had on that prior Monday to get me through the week. Before I exit my vehicle, I reluctantly gather my things, turn off the ignition of my minivan, exhale deeply, and ready myself for the performance I must put on. It's kind of ironic, because my childhood dream was to become an actress.

That seriously just dawned on me! Digressing again...

I really enjoy my work, but it's just so...people-y. Why the hell would I become a cosmetologist if I don't like people? You can't help what you're good at, that's why.

I won't bore you with the details of everyday life in a nail salon, but I can tell you that every day that I show up, I wonder if it'll be my last day there. Much like wondering if every day overseas would be my last. But in this case, I wonder if I'll snap again or at the very least, lay down some serious truth bombs on one of the most trying individuals I've ever met. I wish I could insert an example of what I mean, but truth be told, there are too many and my memory's not all that great, so I guess you just had to be there.

Both my therapist and psychologist have said that it takes courage to face the world everyday knowing how I feel deep inside. That it speaks to my character that I'm willing to risk my own sanity for the sake of providing for my child. That it shows I am brave, fearless, even admirable to just simply show up as jacked up as I am. I said "jacked up," not them.

Well, as wonderful as all that sounds, it is just not how I feel about any of that.

Ever.

That courage feels more to me like fear. The fear of placing myself into the unknown and getting rejected for it. And not even just by strangers, but by people who would call themselves family. It's one thing for strangers to not understand you, but for "family" to never even inquire or even attempt to understand is another betrayal.

Furthermore, the part where it speaks to my character can be negated by the earlier tidbit of information that I gave you stating that I'm NOW A CRIMINAL! Albeit, I've learned that a LOT of veterans have experienced that downfall, but all that proves is that some of us are certainly not the people who should be held in such high regard as we are. Okay fine, there are a select few who have managed to keep their noses squeaky clean and wholeheartedly deserve all of your admiration and respect, but all the ones I know, and not all from the same branch of service, have gone a little...rogue. We were good at one point, though.

And lastly, to believe that I am brave, fearless or admirable, is just an overall silly concept. At best, I take risks.

And not the good kind.

The kind that can either get you safely home at the end of the day, or have you home in a drunken stupor scaring your doggies because Cersei Lannister from Game of Thrones has committed another evil deed and pissed me, I mean you, off for no good reason.

Effing yellow-haired shit.

CHAPTER 13

From Trainee to Airman 2006

Eventually, Sixth Week (really seventh; 0 week to sixth week) of basic training arrived and with it, another proud moment in my Air Force career.

We were finally allowed to wear Blues!

Later on, when it became mandatory on Mondays in 2009 (I know my fellow Airmen remember that), it would become a true pain in the ass. Especially for those who had put on a few pounds over the years and had to buy new uniforms!

But that first time, you couldn't put a price tag on that feeling of accomplishment. It was a privilege that had been earned. The Air Force had allowed us to wear its colors. After so much hard work and mind-effery, that whole week we wore those uniforms with true pride. Mind you, we were thirsty as hell because we couldn't wear our canteens like we could with BDUs anymore, but the overall morale was changed.

We had made it. And all of us together, no less.

Then the moment we never thought would come had arrived. We made it to graduation. Which meant seeing our families again.

And suddenly I was afraid.

I just remember wondering if my mother would be proud of me. Would she finally approve? Would she like what she saw? Hell, would she even recognize me?

Then I saw them. My family. I pretended that I hadn't seen them at first because I hadn't meant to so quickly after we'd been dismissed from the ceremony.

"Wendy! We're over here," my mom yelled in excitement.

My younger brother reached me first and we all hugged. It was a very surreal moment and I can't remember if I cried or not. I had waited for what seemed like forever to see my mother's face again, but I just remember trying to be strong and not like the crybaby on the phone five weeks prior. She was close to tears herself as she hugged me as tightly as she ever has.

"I feel like I'm going to break you in half, you're so small!"

And we all laughed. It was a nice icebreaker because everyone was super nervous.

We ended up going to a San Antonio Spurs game and that was totally and completely insane. At any moment, I expected to see my T.I. jump from around some unforeseen corner and chew me out. I was on edge the whole night. I was with my family again, but I felt so out of place. All I was worried about was keeping my blues clean!

That night, when they dropped me off at my dorm, I was both heartbroken to leave them and relieved to be back with my Air Force sisters.

We all shared our stories of what we'd done that night and what we planned to do the next day since we had two or three days of Base Lib (Liberty). We even got a surprise visit that evening in the day room from the female T.I. that had aided in shaping us into the strong women we had become.

"So how weird was it for you guys to see your families again?"

After nervous laughter, someone raised a hand and answered.

"Ma'am, Airman So & So reports as ordered..."

"No more reporting statements," she interrupted as she waved it off. "We're all Airmen now."

We all looked around at each other, a little teary-eyed. The lady who had been party to making us kiss the floor for the past seven weeks had called us equals.

Talk about mind-blowing.

She went on to tell us that Victoria's Secret was having their famous semi-annual sale for anyone going to the mall the next day and everyone just giggled and continued to share their stories.

"What about you, Flight Chief," someone had asked our appointed leader.

"Well, my family couldn't make it, so I don't really have any plans."

"Then you're coming with me and my family," I'd said without hesitation.

She looked like she could cry, but after all we'd been through, there was no way any of us would celebrate alone. It turned out that quite a few others didn't have any family there either, and more sisters banded together to include them into their plans.

You see, blood or not, we were family. We had all suffered through blood, sweat and tears and it was absolutely unacceptable for anyone to be left behind.

We had pushed each other through push-ups, listened to each other cry ourselves to sleep at night, kept each other awake during countless death-by-power-point briefings, made fun of each other for trying to hide clean socks in dirty clothes for an inspection, reassured each other that we didn't look that bad in those God-awful BCGs (birth control glasses), taken each other's braids down, braided it back up, etc.

The Air Force had instilled in us those core values, after all. Integrity first, Service Before Self, and Excellence in

All We Do.

Before she left us that night, Technical Sergeant Rhodes looked at us with pride. She was probably close to tears herself, but no way was she going to let us see that! But with that last look, we all understood what had transpired that evening.

We had finally become the strong women we were meant to be.

CHAPTER 14

A Little Bit of Freedom 2006

It was now time for the next chapter in our lives: technical training school. A lot of us said our goodbyes and never saw each other again. Sure, we kept in touch for as long as we could, but we all know how that goes.

While mostly everyone else got to leave Lackland for their tech school, I would get to spend the next 13 weeks of my life right around the corner training as a Security Forces member. Lucky for me, I still had my main sister from basic with me and we got through that together too.

After two or three weeks of tech school, we were allowed to go off base! But where to go in the huge city of San Antonio? Well, to the River Center Mall, of course!

We were, after all, still Cali girls at heart.

I remember how excited we were getting off that shuttle! A lot of us hadn't left Lackland AFB since we graduated BMT and were granted Base Lib.

I'm not really sure how, but we ended up at Hooters. And we had linked up with two more of our female tech school counterparts. We'd seen other members of our team, and it was really weird to see them out of their uniforms. They probably felt the same way, because they had barely recognized us either.

Later on, our team had to go to Camp Bullis for survival and tactical skills. Playing war games was all fine and dandy, but when Beanie's sister came to visit her one weekend, we happily packed our overnight bags and welcomed another couple days of freedom. See, even though it was her sister who had come for her, there was no way she was leaving me behind.

Because we were sisters too.

And her actual sister treated me as such without hesitation. I don't remember everything we did, but that is the weekend I fell in love with the Cheesecake Factory!

Thank you, Beanie's sister, for including me that weekend!

When we graduated, though, I'm very sad to say that we didn't even get to say goodbye. I just remember that day being very chaotic, so there was just no time. I'm pretty sure we took pictures and all that, but I never saw her again after that day.

Not to get all sappy, but to go from seeing someone every day, crying and laughing together, pushing each other through those tough times…

And suddenly, that person is simply gone.

She was my sister and I have missed her very much over the years. Thank God for Facebook, though, because we have since reconnected and keep in touch to this day.

I love you, Beanie!!!

CHAPTER 15

Guess Where You're Going 2006

On what had to be the windiest day of my life, I arrived at my first duty station: Ellsworth Air Force Base, South Dakota, home of the 28th Security Forces Squadron. No kidding, even with all of my luggage (you know how Cali girls pack), I was almost swept away into the beautiful Black Hills.

But never mind all that, I was in the "Real Air Force" now!

Not gonna lie, it was a very rough first couple of months not knowing anyone, but eventually of course, things got better.

I don't remember every little thing about my arrival, but I do know that in that first week, maybe even by the third day I was there, I was informed that I would be deploying by fall.

Honestly, I wasn't even mad. I thought it was hilarious, actually, because we had already been warned in tech school. They'd even said "It's not a matter of if you're going to deploy, but when."

So, of course, I called my mom and gave her the fantastic

news as soon as I got released that day. I could tell she was upset by the news and probably wanted to pay a little visit to that recruiter, but hey, it's what I signed up for, right?

Eventually, the time came to get ready for deployment training and we were all slotted into our teams. Myself and another Airman I had become friends with were told that we were going to Afghanistan, but later on, we were both switched at the last minute to replace two others on the team going to Iraq.

It's funny that we call them "teams" because that couldn't be further from the truth.

In retrospect, I hadn't experienced true teamwork since basic and tech school.

We might have all gone to training together, joked and all that together, but when stress levels are high and lives are on the line, you find out real fast who's really on your team.

CHAPTER 16

Back and There Again   2007/2008/2009

Not long after that first deployment, I married, bought my first car, and quite unknown to me, had been pregnant ever since we'd stayed overnight in Baltimore. While on leave, I went back home to California and had a blast. I was just happy to be back with my family and I felt welcomed. Of course, my ego was HUGE after surviving Iraq, and in a sense, I felt untouchable. Like I could do or say anything because, eff you, I could've died multiple times.

I cussed out a Nextel guy (lol, Nextel) because he'd cheated me. I even told a pastor who had deployed as a chaplain to Qatar that he had only been on vacation. Which was pretty messed up, because he was very proud of that achievement. Until I came along, that is.

These were just some of the tell-tale signs of my transformation, but I refused to see them as problems.

I can't remember if it was after the first or second deployment that my mother informed me that I had changed. I believe it was the second, so let's go ahead and fast-forward a little bit to right before that.

I got orders to Dyess AFB, Texas, and in December of

2007, I gave birth to my beautiful and only child, Andreas. There was no one I loved more, even to this day, than that child. I knew in my heart, after surviving certain events, that I would kill anyone or die trying if they meant him any harm.

The following spring, I was informed by the Mobility section of my squadron that my then-husband would be deploying once again and very soon. We hadn't even been back from the first deployment for a full year yet. Folks, yes that is what we signed up for, but we have two choices as dual active duty spouses. We either deploy together, or one after the other. So, I decided to waive my six weeks of maternity leave (which I understand is now 12 weeks. Seriously?!) so that I could be ready to deploy as well. So that our son could know us both at the same time, instead of the other option.

Well, as you can imagine, that stressed me out like no other, and as a result, I was no longer able to breastfeed my own infant.

It was just too much.

And as it turns out, God had mercy and allowed us more time with Andreas. We weren't to leave until fall again. Maybe it was foreshadowing; every fall, my life changes drastically. I'd enlisted in the fall, and deployed twice in the fall. I'm pretty sure I even got my probation sentence in the fall...As a matter of fact, yes, I did, and on the same date as my enlistment, nine years later.

Digressing again...

Anyway, I managed to get my post-prego fat ass back into tip-top shape with the help of two four-week sessions of Fit Camp.

I was ready to go (physically).

Before we left for training, my mother came to Abilene and assumed responsibility for her first grandchild for the next eight months. Andreas wasn't even a year old before I had to leave him.

Needless to say, I missed all of his firsts.

I was in Baghdad getting pictures of him emailed to me and I remember just being so angry. I couldn't even be happy to see that he was in good hands. I hated that I couldn't hold him or see him with my own eyes. I even snapped at my mom. Everyone was subject to my wrath, and there were many of them. If someone looked at me wrong, they were getting my Senior Airman rant at full-blast.

So not only was I dealing with the insurgent attacks this time around, and dumb-ass squadron politics, but I was suffering from separation anxiety from my son. He didn't even know who I was. No matter what pictures I left behind or if he heard my voice over the phone. He did not know that it was me who carried him for nine months, anxiously awaiting his arrival.

I felt like a complete failure for leaving him. Even if it was in service to our country. And both of his parents were gone, so if we had both died (which was certainly a possibility on any given day), he'd have become an orphan. He would've been very well taken care of with $800,000 in life insurance, but he wouldn't have had his parents.

And I just wasn't okay with that, so after we got back, I pushed for my retrain (switching career fields) and wasn't approved for it. When that door closed, I put in for my base of preference and was denied that also because my then-spouse was ineligible. But on a happier note, I made Staff Sergeant!

Yeah, there was no way I was about to reenlist for another four years as an NCO in Security Forces. As crappy as it was being an airman (sometimes), I'd seen how our leaders were treated, and on the flip-side of that, how leaders treated airmen.

And I didn't want to be one of them someday.

Like I said before, it wasn't all bad. And later in life, I would return as a Reservist and become an NCO anyway. It's just that Security Forces has a reputation for eating their own. I did my part and never screwed anyone over, but I could no longer be a part of so many backstabbers and hypocrites.

Yeah, I said it.

And just so you know I'm not exaggerating, let me tell you what another back-office jerk did to get his jollies off.

I don't remember the reason, but I went to Lowe's. I was in uniform, and as I was walking back to my car, I spotted a Master Sergeant from my squadron also walking back to his car with his wife.

And in case you're wondering how I knew it was someone from my squadron, you should know that Security Forces people wear berets. They are meant to serve as a distinction from us to everyone else in the Air Force as law enforcement.

I pretended to not have seen him, because that is what I've grown accustomed to do when I see someone I recognize. I'd rather not be seen by them. But he saw me and decided that it would be a great idea to press the lock button on his key so that the horn would sound once I was close enough to his car.

No big deal, right?

This asshole was part of the "welcome back" committee that greeted us at the airport when we got back from Iraq. He knew where I had just come from and still made the choice to induce fear. But unknown to him, I had already suffered my fair share of assholes and had since learned to suppress any outward ticks. When I turned around, he had this stupid-ass, shit-eating grin on his face and I just looked at him. His response was, "Just making sure you're alright, Troop." His wife kind of gave this nervous half-chuckle, as they got into their car and left.

When I got back in my car, I just sat there for a while. I can't tell you if my hands shook or not, but I was an emotional wreck. My heart pounded; I could barely think, and I didn't know what to do. I wouldn't know until nearly 10 years later that I was having an anxiety attack.

Because my own damn leadership didn't give a single shit about my mental stability.

So, I took my exodus and got my Honorable Discharge from the United States Air Force because I had nothing left to offer.

There was nothing else for them to take. But I didn't know that yet. It took years for me to realize what I'd lost in the process.

CHAPTER 17

You're Not Ready for This
2010/2014/2017

Immediately after separating from active duty, it should come as no surprise that I was once again foolish enough to feel free and in control. No more waking up at the crack of dawn, no more back-office politics, no more deploying, no more missing out on raising my son, and no more anything else that made me become the most disgruntled airman I knew.

But what I neglected to realize was that there was also no more feeling like I belonged somewhere.

It didn't take me long to figure out that I needed to find a new form of employment. Contrary to what the public says about "supporting the troops," that warm and fuzzy saying is non-existent in the hiring process. Unless, of course, you know somebody who can hook you up. I learned that little nugget really quick when I was job hunting. It's not what you know, it's who you know.

Despite having an active security clearance, and the skills I obtained while on active duty, my first job post-military was working at an apartment complex. It took me a good five months to lose my shit and finally cuss the manager smooth out.

Two of the three women working there were the most petty and superficial losers I'd ever known. The manager's lap-dog (one of the two women) took it upon herself to tell the whole staff that one of the tenants had an STD because she'd left her medication in the front office. And the manager earned her stern talking-to from me after she got mad that I wanted to go home for lunch instead of going to a restaurant with everyone else. So while everyone else was going out to eat, she wanted me to stay and answer the phone calls. If you're not fully catching on, as long as I was having lunch with them, I could leave, but since I wanted to eat at home, I had to stay behind. We on board now? Sweet. But believe me, there was plenty that led up to the showdown; that was just the final straw.

I had a number of jobs after serving as an active duty member of the United States Armed Forces...and I never lasted more than five months in any of them. I always had a reason for why the job was wrong for me.

The main one being, I don't belong.

I could not make a career of anything anymore.

Following that debacle, I tried to return to active duty but was unsuccessful. Turns out, I would try twice more over the years and would fail each time. Hmmm, starting to wonder if maybe that ship had simply sailed away.

I mean, didn't I say earlier that I'd had nothing left to give? I'm a slow learner. But I was falling, and fast. I thought the Air Force could do for me again what it had done years before.

It became clear to me that I no longer fit in with the general public. Everyone was strange to me, and worse, I was a stranger to them.

Let's go ahead and talk about those three times I tried my damnedest to go back active. I did manage to go Reserves, but I would never go Active Duty again.

Ever since 2010, I have attempted to reenlist into familiar territory. Every single "no" was for a different reason. The first time, it was because I had a child under the age of 18 while being mil-to-mil. For those of you who are not familiar with that term, it means being married to someone who is also an Active Duty service member. I wonder if they were referring to the same spouse and child that I had while I was still active duty mil-to-mil for half of my enlistment. The child I was separated from on my second deployment. Hmm…

The second attempt wasn't a "no" on their end, but on mine. "Say what?" you might ask. Well, by then it had been five years since my last vacation to Iraq, and by that time, I had become a very angry person with a very short fuse. What you might call a ticking time-bomb. And I had ticktocked myself into becoming a criminal.

My last and final heart-shattering "no" was the worst possible slap in the face that came in the year of 2017. Wait, that's pretty recent! Do I mean to tell you that up until last year I had been trying to get back in? Yes, ma'am and sir.

I have only recently given up that ghost.

I had completed my one year of deferred adjudication. I was 100% forthcoming with the recruiter about my checkered past, but that wasn't actually the reason I was given the no-go. I'm not sure if you guys are ready for this, so prepare to either throw this book or tablet across the room, or just bow your head in angry silence. Maybe it'll be funny to you, I don't know. But anyway, I couldn't get back into my beloved Air Force because I had been diagnosed with PTSD!

Wait, so the reason I have PTSD in the first place wouldn't let me come back? The reason I don't fit in anywhere else in the world is casting me out? To where? "Who cares, just not with us! Sayonara, Sucka!" I wasn't even allowed to reenlist as a reservist. A weekend warrior.

So that was the last time I begged my beloved to take me back.

Obviously, I had become damaged goods and was no longer worthy. A better person would believe that everything happens for a reason. But I am not better.

I am bitter.

And now you poor souls are stuck with me. I could apologize for that, but nah, I'm good.

CHAPTER 18

Some 'Splaining to Do   2014/2017

Would you guys like to play a quick game of catch-up? I've said things like "then-husband," and "I was diagnosed with PTSD," and you weren't even given the slightest bit of explanation of when or how or anything.

Well, it's pretty simple. For one, "then-husband" means I got divorced, so that takes care of that. I have given up on many other relationships I had in the past as well.

Both family and alleged friends.

Like I said before, no one understands, so I keep my distance. Plus, I really don't like fake-ass people, and I find that most people are just that. Or at least don't have good intentions. And if anyone who knows me read that and got offended, you're probably one of those fake-ass people, so too-da-loo.

As far as the diagnosis goes, I finally reached a point in my life where I knew something had to change. And no, it wasn't even after jail. I decided to put an end to the endless cycle of trying to fix myself. Because how the eff can the problem fix the problem?

It took me much too long to figure that out.

So, I finally visited my local Veteran's Services office and filed my claim for disability. For some stupid reason, I wasn't prepared to have to narrate my overseas experience. I was absolutely horrified that I'd have to relive those nightmares. But I did it. I had to. Things that I hadn't acknowledged out loud in years were on those papers. It should come as no surprise that I was mentally effed all the way up after that. It's actually the reason I decided to write this book.

I began to get angry all over again. I began to drink.

A lot.

And I could feel myself spiraling out of control, so I did something else that completely freaked me out. I contacted my therapist (the one I had to see after getting arrested). I simply said "I think I need to start seeing you again." I'm not sure how she knew that it was me years later, but she did and she replied very cheerfully that she'd be happy to help. Or she just figured it was obviously a past-patient that needed her assistance.

So, for the first time, I began to fight my demons instead of giving in to them or hiding from them.

Following that, the VA scheduled my appointment to see a psychologist to determine whether or not I really had PTSD. I'm sure you can all guess that outcome. Once again, I had to describe everything I experienced and it was no easier that time. It is no picnic admitting that something is wrong with you. Or that you know you're not like everyone else. That you have to pretend on a daily basis. That even though you take showers, put on clothes that fit and match, sometimes put makeup on your face, or even occasionally smile and can hold a conversation, doesn't mean that everything is kosher. The surface isn't the problem. Only through digging deeper will you see that a person can very well be on the verge of self-destruction from their own mental instability.

There you have it. Catch-up achieved.

Now I'm a single mother doing the best I can by my son. My main mission in life is for him to know that I will always fight for him. That I will always choose the hard path if it will make it easier for him. He will know in the end that his mother loves him, because many people do not have such a privilege.

Many people take blood for granted and the lack of it for an easy ticket out.

CHAPTER 19

When Change Causes Failure 2017

"They've diagnosed me with PTSD."

I'd sent the text message to my "mom" a few days after I had seen the psychologist appointed by Veterans Affairs for my disability claim. Although I'd known for a long time that something was wrong with me, the actual diagnosis had served as another blow.

"Okay."

Point blank. No whats, hows or whens. Not to mention, an "Are you okay?"

As I stared at her shitty, uncaring reply, I finally came to the realization that the mother I had once known was gone. Just like the child she had once known and loved was gone too.

Andreas was truly the only family I had now.

I reflected back on a previous conversation I'd had with my estranged mother when I told her of my decision to finally seek help and apply for disability. At the time, my life was in shambles and my son needed a real mother. Not one who pretended to be okay all the time in order to reassure him that he was in the best possible hands.

One who could set aside her pride for his sake.

"Well, what if you apply for disability and that messes up your chances of getting another VA Loan? Because isn't that the same thing as suing the military? Wouldn't they take it out on you by not giving you a new loan? How else would you be able to get a house in California?"

Those are legit, no exaggerations, the questions my mother asked me in regards to seeking the help that superseded a stupid-ass new house. As if getting a new house should take precedence over my mental health. And furthermore, why in the hell would I want to move back to a state where not a single familial soul could give a shit about where or how I am?

Needless to say, I did not take her advice and began the process of becoming something more than what I had become.

I had allowed eleven years to go by without seeking any help for my condition. And in those eleven years, much devastation had occurred in my life.

I won't consider my getting divorced one of those devastations because honestly, it was doomed from the get-go. I mean, shit, we met in Iraq on my first deployment, and I just wanted my own family so I just jumped at the first opportunity. It was awful for my son to endure, though. And I do feel badly for him on that one.

Throughout those years, I had become a very angry person. And resentful, and downright alienated from the world.

I felt as though no one understood what I was going through, that everyone judged me. And not just judged me, I felt they were against me.

With that in mind, it should come as no surprise that I would eventually become a criminal. And not just any kind of criminal, a felon.

I lost many friends along the way. People I had known for years I decided that I no longer needed them in my life because their intentions were suddenly unclear to me. Family members as well because their intentions were crystal clear: to isolate their changed "loved" one.

That one I've made peace with, because family has been letting me down since I can remember. To me, family means the people who are with you no matter what you're going through.

Through counseling and talking to other vets, I am finally getting my self-worth back.

Instead of seeing myself as flawed for being cautious, I am grateful to be a person who will not trust just anyone who calls themselves a friend or family.

I like that I will not settle. That even in my loneliest, out of place moments, I will still refuse to be surrounded by people who do not have honest intentions.

Even though I've gone through some traumatic events, I remember myself. I have always been a fighter and I've always stood my ground. Despite, no, in spite of everything that's happened, I still believe in myself.

The war might be over, but the fight is not.

CHAPTER 20

A Change in Scenery 2018

To this day, I consider a knock on my door to be a probable threat. My four dogs bark wildly each time, providing the perfect distraction for me to quietly tip-toe and peer out of the peephole at whoever could be the danger to me and my son's safety. The doggies are just doing their job, oblivious to my hyper-vigilance. But maybe, and this would be much worse, they have learned to feed off my suspicious tendencies.

Even after determining that the person on the other side of the door is no threat, many times I still do not answer. In fact, nine times out of ten, I will not.

Other than the door-knocking, when my son is home, I pretend to be normal. I open the blinds and I begin our day. Just like any other mother would do, because that's what a regular mom does. But if Andreas is gone, I watch firestick all day in complete darkness. Curtains drawn and blinds shut tight, with a mixed drink within arm's reach.

I do my best for Andreas' sake, but if he's gone due to court ordered visitation, I find myself feeling guiltily relieved of his absence. Why? Because it's exhausting feigning normalcy all the time. I can't sink into depression with him around to worry about dear old mom. Despite my efforts, he must still sense something is wrong because he often asks me if I'm okay.

Well, shit.

And am I saying that I want to be depressed? No, it means that it's important to be honest about your feelings, instead of tucking them underneath as tightly as BMT hospital bedsheet corners.

Even with the therapy I receive, I'm still trapped in my thoughts. Everyone is an enemy. Sometimes, even my child. What if he's telling his father what a failure I am? That I get angry, sad, emotional, or even worse, that I'm planning our exodus out of Abilene? I wasn't given any geographical restrictions in the final divorce decree, but I'm always fearful that one false move could ruin everything.

Just as sure as I'm sitting here writing this, I know that it is time for us to leave Abilene, possibly even Texas. So, for that reason, my son and I, accompanied by my bestie from cosmetology school, took an impromptu road trip to Tucson, Arizona, to check out a house I'd seen on Trulia.

The trip was a great success, and although I didn't end up moving there, the prospect of moving to a new place kept me going. I mean, naturally, I ended up telling some random lady off for not minding her own effing business, but other than that, a good time was had.

I ended up moving to Maryland instead. About ten minutes away from Baltimore, where my son was conceived, as coincidental as that seems.

And I haven't looked back since.

I still have my days that are truly awful, but I continue to fight. Sometimes it feels like all of my life is just a constant struggle for survival, but I'm here.

And I'll be here for as long as I can.

Why?

Because I am willing to fight until the end.

CHAPTER 21

In Conclusion

I'm not sure if I'll ever be what's considered normal again. I've asked, but who really knows except God? All I can do is continue to seek treatment and keep fighting for survival.

I know one thing for sure, though: I wouldn't trade my experiences for anything.

Why? Because I truly believe that it was all for a purpose.

To help others who think they're alone in the way they feel. To bring them out of the darkness because that's not a fun place to be. The mind is no joke and the Enemy rejoices every time we give in to those thoughts. I needed to turn my nightmares into hope for someone else.

So for those of you reading this and are now having second thoughts of joining the Armed Forces (or someone you love from joining), please do not have those second thoughts. I meant what I said before. Serving is my biggest achievement. Even knowing what I know now and how I turned out, I would still do it all over again.

It's just that I earned the right to talk shit.

My intention is not to deter a single soul from becoming

an Airman, Soldier, Marine, Sailor, or Coast Guard member. I simply wanted to share my experiences in case someone with similar ones thought they were alone.

My only piece of advice is to not shut people out like I did...um, do. Well, the people who matter, at least. Tell your family or very close friends what you go through instead of holding it all in until you're convinced that there's no way they could ever "get you." Years will go by and you can lose a lot of loved ones without going to a single funeral.

My thoughts and prayers are with my fellow vets always, and I hope you find comfort in knowing that. Many of you have suffered much worse than I have, but our results seem to be the same: feeling like we're cut-off from the world, among many other things.

Also, the absence of physical scars doesn't mean that we are not injured. Our wounds are still very real. Do not underestimate the damage that the mind can do when it's left untreated. We can't hide or be in denial anymore. We should come out of the shadows and help each other get through these rough times.

We should truly be a team.

And I still believe that we have much to contribute through our experiences. I mean, you won't catch me on the next deployment, unfortunately, but there's still plenty for us to do.

But more importantly, get the help that you know you need. No matter what anyone else has to say about it.

God bless each and every one of you brave souls.

EPILOGUE

But What About Love?

I have only experienced one relationship where it was totally innocent and carefree. I laugh to myself thinking about it, because there is no love purer than your first one. I don't think we ever forget those. Especially if you still keep in touch and life has taken you places where that's really the last time you remember being completely happy. Most people have long-since let go of that person, but if you haven't discovered by now, I'm not most people.

I swear you guys won't believe me, but I literally just got a text from that very person telling me for the millionth time to finish this book...

Anyway, we didn't last long because he answered our nation's call while I was still feeling like somebody special in my AFJROTC cadet uniform.

When September 11th happened, I remember how worried I was about him. I remember everything about that day. How my hair was styled, what I was wearing, and which class I was in when I found out. But most memorable to me, is that I remember praying for him (back when prayer was okay on school grounds) and being completely afraid for his life. I've never told him that, but I suppose the jig's up now.

Little did I know that five years later, I would be experiencing similar traumatic life-changing events that he did when our nation was attacked that fateful day. Maybe that's the reason it's so hard for me to let go.

I feel that he's the only person in the world who truly understands me. Knows the person I used to be and the person I am now.

We knew each other before the wars. Long ago, we were crazy kids in love. Now we're just freaking crazy.

I wonder if a couple of crazy vets could find that missing link in each other.

Wouldn't that just be freaking fantastic?

Yeah, I thought so too.

Thanks for reading.

Acknowledgments

Of course, I have to thank God for giving me every single tool I needed to write this book. Down to the ability to even put words together that somewhat make sense. All of my life experiences, the people placed in my life before and after, were all for a purpose. Whether those people are no longer in my life, or stuck it out and are still with me, I am thankful.

Thank God for Top Golf and that silent auction that led me to Mrs. Judy Watters and Franklin Scribes. It's been about two years now, but I'm finally making good on that deal. Regardless of my many breaks and head-on collisions with brick walls, you always treated me like an equal and had encouraging words for me, so thank you.

To all of my fellow bro's & sisters-in-arms. Every branch. You are all one of a kind.

To my very special sisters-in-arms Heather Hively, Kristy Horton and, Kathryn Bean. I love you guys so much. Kristy, you know you're my big sister, but I will never let that OC pepper spray incident go! Heather and Beanie, I am just so damn happy that we were able to reconnect after all these years.

I'm grateful for all the lovely ladies of BIB that I met on Facebook before I quietly bowed out when it got wayyyyyy out of hand! Thanks for the reminder that we're all scattered across the globe sharing, laughing and crying while struggling with similar issues. Special thank you to Meranda, Amy and Melkys for your unconditional support.

Thank you to Erin Smith and my ex-adult babysitter, for suffering through reading my first attempts at writing a novel. Maybe Re/Bonded will see the light of day in the future, but we'll just stick a pen in that one for now.

Dr. Linda Spetter, you believed in me at an extremely vital time in my life. And from day one, you called me a writer. I will always be grateful for the brief time I had you as a mentor.

To Jeanette and Sha'Destiny for just being freaking fantabulous friends. Even from a distance.

To Jon, for practically forcing me to get off my ass and write this book. Actually, I'm on my ass writing it, but you get what I'm saying.

To Ms. Pam. Words cannot express how grateful I am for your generosity. You really are an angel visiting us lost souls on Earth. I pray that you know what a blessing you are. I may have moved, but I have not and will not ever forget you.

To those of you who stuck it out and read this thing all the way, thank you ever so much. You could be reading something epic instead like Harry Potter, but you're here with me.

To Brynda, Speedy and Shadow. My absolutely irreplaceable fur babies that couldn't make the move with us. Not a day goes by that I don't think of you and how much you would have loved our new home. I can only pray that your new owners love you just as much as we do.

To my beautiful big sister who wasted no time rescuing me from an awful life of pure loneliness. No one could've done it but you. Thank God we've found each other again.

And last, but not least, to my beautiful son. You are the reason I still have the ability to fight for life. It is by no means easy, but you make it worth it. I hope someday you'll understand why I'm so hard on you. I want you to be prepared for the beauty and the ugliness of this world. But in due time, I suppose.

Andreas, I love you more than anything.
Also, close your freaking mouth!

I love you all,
Wendy

Some Security Forces "Humor..."

Don't get me wrong, that awkward feeling we all have when you guys tell us "Thank you for your service" really does touch us. We just don't know how to respond really. Most of us will politely say "You're welcome, Sir" or "Ma'am."

We do, however (well, women), absolutely hate it when men and women alike assume that it was our husband who served. Yep, even in the 21st century, people will still give credit to the imaginary (or real) man in our lives before they accept that a woman could actually serve her country.

Tsk, tsk.

Before I really close, here's some large and very important "don'ts" when encountering a gate guard. If you happen to be getting your ID inspected at an installation gate, do not, I repeat do NOT say any combination of these words:

1. Stay Warm. Okay, we know it's cold and those words are not going to magically make us warmer. I mean, did you include hot chocolate, tea, or blankets, thicker gloves, etc. along with those carefully-chosen thoughtful words? Because how else would we "stay warm?" Just wondering...

2. Stay Cool. Just like before, your words will not change the weather. Also, did you bring a nice cold gallon of water (the best dollar you could spend for a gate guard) in order for that "coolness" to be accomplished? No? Then you must realize now what an unrealistic request that is.

3. You guys really have to work today? Okay, so if you're rolling through our gate, OF FREAKING COURSE, we're working. Did you think the fact that it's Christmas matters? Let's say it together: Nope!

4. Why is the gate/other lane closed/traffic stopped? Let's go ahead and assume it's for everyone's safety, and we're not just getting our bored jollies off like the aforementioned jerk Master Sergeant. Thanks very kindly.

5. Happy Friday! Oh, yes, because it's Friday, that means we're off for the weekend too, right? WRONG! Moving on...

SUPER BONUS TIP: If you pull up to the gate and decide to be major male genitalia and not greet the poor soul that opened their mouth to say "Good morning/afternoon/evening, Sir/Ma'am" to your punk ass, you better believe that person will suddenly chipper up and take pleasure in taking for-effing-ever before they give you back your ID. We're all in this together, people. Don't let America's 1% feel like their service was in vain because you're pissed that you're up "so early." Guess what? They were up at 0300 and didn't get to say "Good Morning" to their spouse or babies or even drop them off at school like you most likely got to!! Jerk...